MONDO BIZARRO

BY PIRARO

Chronicle Books · San Francisco

Printed in the United States of America.
ISBN: 0-87701-711-5
Distributed in Canada by Raincoast Books, 112 East Third Avenue,
Vancouver B.C., V5T 1C8

Chronicle Books, 275 Fifth Street, San Francisco, CA 94103

Mondo thanks to the Semi-Official Bizarro
Canadian Fan Club and Motor Oil Company.
Marty, John, Ken and Tony.
And Willie the newspaper guy.

All my work is dedicated to the six Ks in my life, most especially the
inimitable Kalin, who keeps me motivated, teaches me history,
and made me see the inherent superiority of women. With the following
exceptions: The first two words of the far left panel on page 72 are
dedicated to my extended family. All the punctuation on pages 18
through 25 is dedicated to my friends. The hands and feet of all the
characters on pages with a zero in their number are dedicated to the
fine folks at CatPak, StatCat, and The Mews Design Lab in Dallas.

BOMC offers recordings and compact discs, cassettes
and records. For information and catalog write to
BOMR, Camp Hill, PA 17012.

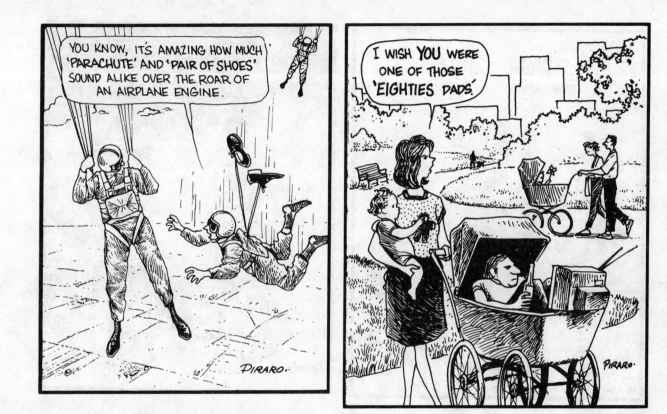

3

START AT BACK OF BOOK
& FLIP THIS CORNER →
FORWARD WITH LEFT THUMB.

4

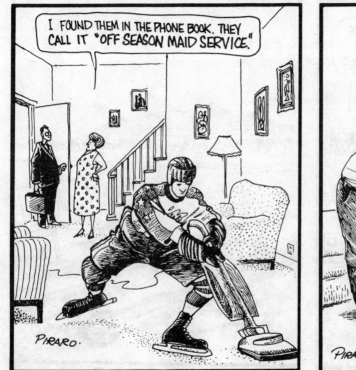

6

8

9

13

15

27

28

29

33

36

38

39

41

42

44

49

Dear Santa,

Doubtless you remember our meeting of December 3rd last, wherein I related my undying fascination with the TXJ 2000 Space Cruiser. While I was pleased to find it under the tree on Christmas morning, I now find that my original infatuation for it has diminished considerably.

Please advise me as to your current return and/or exchange policy.

As ever,

65

72

76

82

90

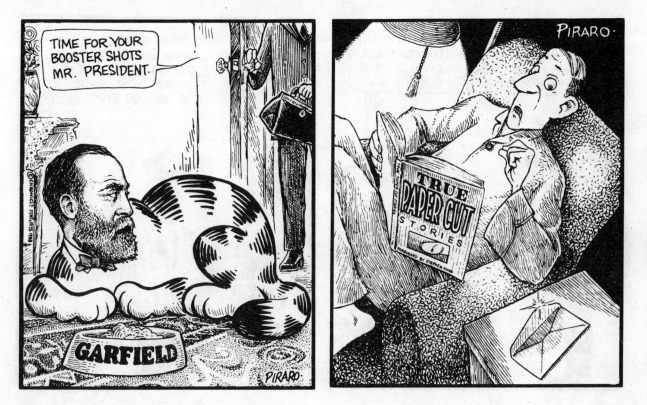

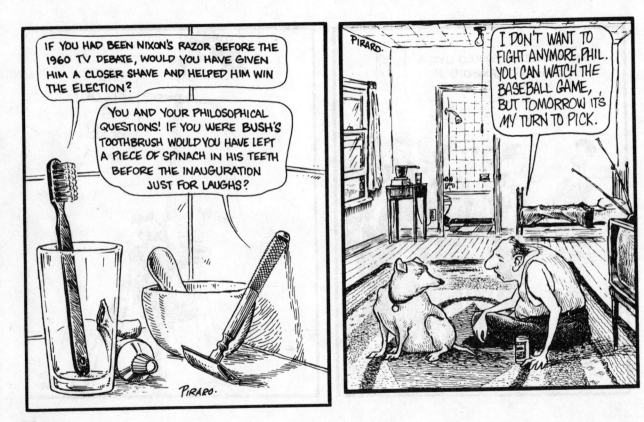

99

ABOUT THE ARTHUR

Perhaps the greatest virtuoso conductor of the 20th century, Arturo (a funny Italian way of spelling Arthur) Toscanini was born in 1867 in Parma, Italy. He studied at the conservatories of Parma and Milan, intending to become a cellist, but became a conductor because the equipment was easier to carry.

Toscanini had several good jobs, including musical director of La Scala, in Milan, and of the Metropolitan Opera in New York City. Though no definitive research exists on the subject, it is probably safe to assume he liked Italian food.

Arturo (Arthur) Toscanini died in 1957 in New York, at the age of 90. At no time during his life was he known for drawing a syndicated cartoon feature, but he lived a pretty interesting life anyway.

START AT FRONT OF BOOK
& FLIP THIS CORNER
← FORWARD WITH RIGHT
THUMB AND LAUGH.